, Megan McNeil

from

06

Postcards from France

Postcards from France

MEGAN McNEILL LIBBY

HarperPaperbacks

🔥 HarperPaperbacks
A Division of HarperCollins*Publishers*
10 East 53rd Street, New York, N.Y. 10022-5299

ISBN: 0-06-101169-X

HarperCollins®, 🔥 ®, and HarperPaperbacks™
are trademarks of HarperCollins*Publishers* Inc.

Postcards from France was originally published as
a series of articles in *The Ridgefield Press*, and in
book form by North River Press in 1995.

First HarperPaperbacks printing: March 1997
Designed by Lili Schwartz

Library of Congress Cataloging-in-Publication Data

Libby, Megan McNeil.
   Postcards from France/Megan McNeill Libby.
      p.   cm.
   ISBN 0-06-101169-X
   1. Libby, Megan McNeil—Journeys—France—Valence
   (Drôme) 2. Valence (Drôme, France)—Social life and
   customs. 3. American characteristics, French—Humor.
   I. Title.
DC801.V2L53 1997
944'.98—dc20   96-30924
                                                CIP

Printed in the United States of America

Visit HarperPaperbacks on the World Wide Web at
http://www.harpercollins.com/paperbacks

❖ 10 9 8 7 6 5 4 3 2 1

Dedication

Every artist, whether a writer, a dancer, a musician, or a painter, requires stimulation in order to create. Something she sees or hears or experiences inspires her to create something new, something of value.

Obviously France was my inspiration—the country, its people, its culture. And what an inspiration it was! A kid could do a lot worse than France. But I never would have spent my junior year of high school in France if it had not been for the American Field Service (AFS), which I knew there as Vivre Sans Frontières, or life without borders. With AFS, teens from all over the world learn to cross over borders of all kinds—the actual physical borders between countries, cultural borders, linguistic borders, personal borders. Without AFS, I never would have had the experience of becoming a French teenager for a year, met the people I wrote about, traveled to the places I described, and learned to speak another language. Without AFS I would not have known the satisfaction of doing something which at first seemed impossible and out of my reach. In short, I would have had no reason to write the articles which evolved into this book, and I wouldn't have become the person who could write this book.

So I dedicate this book to AFS and in doing so I acknowledge a global community whose members include persons from 155 countries. People from all races, religions, and ethnic backgrounds participate in programs designed to foster tolerance and understanding. In this goal, AFS succeeds admirably.

Table of Contents

Foreword

I first met Megan Libby when she came to my office at *The Ridgefield Press* in the late summer of 1994. She explained that she was to be an exchange student in France during the coming school year and volunteered to write about her experiences for our newspaper. I agreed, but based on my past experience with young people who volunteer to write, I didn't expect much, if anything. High-school kids who want to write, or think they want to write, are plentiful. Few are willing to do the work involved in producing something good enough to be run without apology in the newspaper.

I was pleasantly surprised when my first "Postcard from France," as Megan called her column, arrived. Not only had she written something, she had done it very well. Her copy was lively, interesting, and focused not simply on her individual adventure, but on what France and its culture looked like from a young American's viewpoint.

Once a month, I received a column Megan wrote based

on her experience as an AFS student in France. The columns kept getting better. Megan had a good idea what would be interesting to the folks back home, and a natural sense of how to use her personal experience as an exchange student as a vehicle for contrasting the two societies. I began to look forward to Megan's columns. Our proofreader, who reads just about everything in eight weekly papers, looked forward to them as well.

In all, Megan submitted twelve columns over the course of her year in France, one for each month she was gone. It is interesting to see how Megan has edited these columns and pulled them all together to form a book with the title—what else?—*Postcards from France.*

My proofreader and I will miss those columns from France, but we will still have a chance to watch Megan develop as a writer, both in her book and in future columns. Megan will be covering the high school for us during her senior year and, again, turning in a bimonthly column for *The Ridgefield Press.*

Postcards from France is a vivid look at France and a fascinating glimpse into how a year in a different culture is a trial by fire that broadens the outlook and develops the inner resources of a bright young American.

Macklin Reid, Editor
The Ridgefield Press

ONE

Prêt à Partir?
(READY TO GO?)

It all started innocently enough. I was a pretty typical fifteen-year-old high-school sophomore, living in Fairfield County, Connecticut. That translates to mean I had it pretty good. I lived in a nice house in an historic New England town with my parents, my younger brother, and a Labrador retriever. My older sister, an attorney, lived in Chicago with her husband and baby daughter. I had doting grandparents, aunts, uncles, and cousins. Not everyone was completely sane, but no one had been put away, and most of us could act pretty normal most of the time. I went to a good public high school, where I got good grades, had a great group of friends, played sports, joined clubs, volunteered, enjoyed art and music, and partied enthusiastically wherever and whenever possible.

Was I happy? Certainly not. I was fifteen, after all. I had a constitutional right as an American to want more, even if I didn't know what I wanted more of. My days were boring and predictable. Most of my classes seemed irrelevant. The only subjects I was really interested in were English, French, and art. I loved to write and to draw, and I wanted to actually speak French. Naturally I knew that in order to achieve any of these goals I would have to do the boring and predictable and repetitive stuff. Right then, however, I wanted to do something exciting and unique. I should admit up front to being a risk-taker, even a thrill-seeker. I love the jolt of adrenaline that comes from doing something terrifying.

According to my family, I was born that way. At one year of age, I piled up the stuffed animals in my crib, climbed up on their backs, and launched myself headfirst over the bars and onto the floor. By fifteen months I was walking on the kitchen counters and swinging from the freezer door. I had a genius for getting up on high places and being unable to get down safely. At two I had graduated from climbing on kitchen counters and chain-link fences to removing window screens and strolling on rooftops during nap time.

And then my baby brother was born. He cried all night for a year. My dad left town a lot, and my mom was pretty much over the edge. It got easier and easier to slip away from the house, down the block, across streets and out into the big world. I particularly liked the monkey bars at the school playground and looking in at the big kids in kindergarten and first grade. But somebody always called the police, and after a while they didn't have to ask me where I lived anymore. They just picked me up and drove me home. When I was finally old enough to get inside the school and swing legally from the monkey bars, we moved to Connecticut.

The move wasn't all bad. There was no block to play on, but there was a whole forest full of trees, giant boulders, ponds, even a "haunted house" on the other side of the mountain, where I could press my face against the window and run away screaming when the "monsters" moved around inside. Life was good. But after about five years, the trees weren't tall enough anymore, and the only one left who was scared of the haunted house was my little brother. The thrill was gone. My parents did their best. After striking out with dance, gymnastics, and softball, they tried a local camp which specialized in excitement and adventure. No clay pots, sing-alongs, or plays for Mountain Workshop. We climbed mountains, rappelled off cliffs, went caving, canoeing, white-water rafting, and roaring around on dirt bikes. The only problem was it didn't last all year long.

What I'm coming around to is that I think what my life lacked at fifteen, what I was looking for, was danger, the thrill of the unknown. I wasn't far enough over into the fast lane. And then a former friend who was understandably sick of my depression —(the French would say *malaise*)—told me to stop complaining and do something, take charge of my life, make a change. She steered me to an evening meeting of a group called AFS (American Field Service). They specialized in sending American kids to faraway places, for the summer, a semester, even a year. They placed you with a local family; you learned the language and saw the world. That was it! I'd go to France for a year, take all my courses in French, become bilingual, see Europe, ski the Alps, SCUBA dive in the Mediterranean; the possibilities were limitless.

I told my parents. They agonized for about fifteen minutes over losing me for a whole year, then sent in their check. That was in November. By April I had serious cold feet.

I drove everyone crazy. On Monday I was going. By Tuesday I was staying home. On Wednesday I reconsidered. Would I like my new family? Would they like me? Would I ever have any friends? Just how good was my French, anyhow? Could I leave my dog for a whole year? My boyfriend belonged to the stay-at-home camp. My parents, by this time several thousand dollars into the experiment, weren't speaking to him. For the first time in my life, I was scared to death, and I *didn't* like it.

And that's how it happened that on August 31, 1994, I flew to Paris with fifty other AFS students from all over the USA. An AFS representative met our flight and whisked us off to a youth hostel in a Paris suburb. All I saw of the City of Light was a distant image of the Eiffel Tower, growing quickly more distant. The next morning, after little food and less sleep, I found myself at the train station with a ticket in my mouth and all my worldly possessions in two duffel bags at my side. I think it was at that moment that I realized the enormity of what I had done. I had left everything and everyone I'd ever known and loved behind for a year and was about to step on the Bullet Train into the unknown.

And I was alone. I didn't know whether to laugh or cry, so I sat down on my bags and did a little of both, got up, wiped my nose on my sleeve, and dragged my bags to the train. I had to drag my duffel bags because I couldn't lift them; they exceeded the forty-four-pound weight limit suggested by AFS by at least twenty pounds. The shoes and boots were the problem. I couldn't decide which to take, so I packed them all.

Three hours later I arrived in Valence. My host family was waiting at the train station to welcome me. I recognized my "mom" from the photographs she'd sent. The family was warm and welcoming. I was exhausted and hungry. I could tell they were asking me questions about my trip, but I might as well have been on another planet for all I could understand or say. Surely, it is not possible to speak English that fast. Eventually my new family must have realized that I was either an idiot, very tired, or both, and they put me to bed.

When I woke up the next morning I had achieved full-blown culture shock, but during my first week in France I had enough temporary moments of alertness to make a few observations. The most important one was that I had a lot of preconceptions about France and French people, and most of them were wrong. French people are not unfriendly, rarely rude, and, as a rule, they do not dislike Americans. Rather, the French I met in those last days of summer were polite and easygoing. They have a saying: "*Ce n'est pas grave.*" It means, "no problem," "don't worry about it," "it's not important." And they mean it. I spilled red wine all over a woman's dress and all she said was, *"ce n'est pas grave."* My mother would think it was very "grave" indeed.

In the beginning at least, the French seemed much more laid-back than we are in New England. They spend hours lounging at outdoor cafés, talking about whatever interests them. Politics interests them, and current events. They are extremely well informed, at least about events in their own country. I decided I could get used to this life, especially the part where they lounge around, sipping the wine just in from the harvest, and talking into the long evening. Eventually, I imagined, I might even be able to join in the talk. For the time being, however, I had to be satisfied with listening and watching these exotic, different people. I noticed that young women do shave their legs, they have heard of putting ice in drinks, and most people shower daily, but they're in and out quickly because water costs so much.

The French do, I learned, have a different concept of hygiene, however. They think Americans are positively crazy and obsessive about cleanliness. It's OK to smell like a human, they think, and not like a bar of soap and a bottle of mouthwash. And they think a little hair under the arms is natural, even sexy. They also have some crazy notions about us. My first French acquaintance, Anne, was astonished to learn that Americans actually drink water, like French food, and do not eat hamburgers, hot dogs, and fries every day, washed down by gallons of Coca-Cola.

One assumption turned out to be completely true, though, and that is that the French live to eat. Food is absolutely central to life in France, and eating is very important, as is talking about eating when you aren't actually doing it. But I saw few fat people during my year in France. That may be because everywhere they go, they walk or ride bikes, whether they're four years old or seventy-four. All that food seems to give them a lot of energy. Not me. After lunch—the big meal of the day—I was paralyzed, and they eat big dinners, too.

At first I bulked up, because I thought I had to keep up with the consumption of my fellow diners, who often ate three-course meals at lunch and dinner, with wine and both cheese *and* a sweet dessert. I watched women under five feet tall and ninety-five pounds pack away meals that would've been a challenge to a truck driver. Gradually, my body adjusted to the onslaught of food, and I actually lost weight. This was a strange phenomenon, and I cannot explain it, especially since the fat content of my diet easily tripled at the same time as my intake doubled. Jenny Craig would have a lot of happy clients if she could package the French secret to weight control—eat as much as you possibly can as often as you can, while consuming as many grams of fat as you can get your hands on and lose twenty pounds in ten months. I'll never know how the French do it, but I think the real reason I lost weight was the French language. Yes, it is a beautiful language. It is also extremely difficult to speak French well. I was determined to learn the language and to speak it without an American accent. I burned up a lot of extra calories with the effort of trying so hard every day and still managing to have a life. Actually, I *didn't* have a life for several months, and I was still weak from nervous exhaustion all the time. I probably burned up five hundred calories a day just wrestling with the letter "R." One of the biggest shocks I had to deal with in those first weeks was the realization that nothing about my year in France was going to be easy.

TWO

Je Parle

(I SPEAK)

he only pastime the French like better than eating is talking.

The French seem to have a lot to say about everything. There is constant, animated conversation. These people *never* stop talking. I had heard the phrases "culture shock" and "language barrier" before I came to France, but I had no idea just how shocking, just what a big barrier, it is to have a lot to say and to be unable to say very much at all. Worse yet, for the first month, I didn't understand much either unless the speaker took pity on me and slowed down, way down. *"Parlez doucement, s'il vous plait,"* I said, like a parrot with one phrase, as I tapped wildly on my little language converter. But *doucement* shouldn't even be in the language. They don't know what it means. I had completed two years of high-school French, in addition to a year in middle school and one class a week after school in fourth and fifth grades. I also took Latin for two years, and later that would become helpful in reading the language. Modern French has obvious roots in ancient Latin. I enjoyed French in school. I had an ear for the accent and rhythm of it, and did well in my classes without all that much effort. *Pas grave*, I thought. No problem.

Well, maybe a problem at first, but I'll catch on quickly. Wrong. Terribly, horribly wrong. What every American high-school student knows, but doesn't know, because our American teachers are kind people who want us to love a foreign language and do well, is that the French do not believe in final consonants. They are there at the end of most words purely for decorative purposes. French is a beautiful language, after all. Sometimes you throw a final consonant in when the next word begins with a vowel, or under certain other specific conditions, but this is more to be devious and contrary than anything else. And the native French speaker rattles on at about four times the speed of any French teacher you ever had. What you hear is a river of sound: lovely, but utterly unintelligible. The French invented slurred speech, then turned it into an art form.

In the beginning, after about twelve hours of intense concentration, during which I understood every fourth word, my brain would just shut down. Sometimes I would see mouths moving all around me, but I couldn't hear anything at all. Sometimes I heard noise, but no recognizable words at all.

Over the course of a year, I lived with two host families, which is another story, but my first host mother was a retired English teacher. She spoke perfect English, with a British accent. The rule was that we spoke only French at home, however. And this was a good rule. If she had given me half a chance, I would have bombarded her with English. I am an extrovert, and I have never been at a loss for words. For the first month I was angry all the time because I couldn't make myself understood. I stamped my foot, and once I even threw my trusty little translator down on the floor and walked away in a grand, dramatic gesture of impatience. Temperamentally, I was not well suited to this part of the experiment.

By the beginning of October things were better. Sometimes I understood an entire complex sentence at top speed, with clauses, adverbs, adjectives, and tense changes. Then I got so impressed with myself that I missed the next three sentences entirely. My head pounded every night. I had to escape to my room, put my earphones on, and listen to my American music just to connect again with something familiar and comforting. In the morning I ran a mile before breakfast to prepare myself for the trauma of the coming day.

And this was just the horror of socializing. School was devastating. I was assigned to the lycée Emile Loubet and placed in the *"Première"* level, where everyone is gearing up to take the "BAC" (Baccalaureate exams). By the time students get to this level in their schooling, there is no one left who has a bad attitude or isn't capable of doing the work. They are tested regularly and rigorously, and those who don't pass either don't continue or enter a trade school. The BAC is a written exam which covers every subject taught. Your score determines whether and where you qualify to go to a university. The kids say, "School is life and life is school," and they mean it. Any French child under age eighteen is expected to devote all his time and energy to achieving the highest possible grades. I keep saying to myself, "*pas grave,*" but the academic situation for me was clearly grave.

I was trade-school material.

My courses at the lycée were French literature and composition, English, chemistry, physics, biology, French history, and art. In the beginning they signed me up for a math class and Latin, too. I had just enough brain function left after a week to figure out that something had to go. Translating Latin to English to French was the road to madness, so that was the first to go. Math followed because I preferred to fail other subjects. At lycée Emile Loubet there were two principals. They were polite and pleasant to the foreign students and have accepted AFS kids before. In fact, there was another AFS girl at the school at the same time, from Maine. We were told that it is normal to be completely lost in the classroom for about three months. Not to worry, eventually something "clicks" in the brain and those who try hard do well by the second semester. No orientation was offered. We were left to sink or swim. After two weeks there was no question in my mind; I was drowning.

Most of my teachers were friendly, but none went out of their way to be helpful. Occasionally, one would ask, "*C'est bon?*" It wasn't "*bon*" at all, so I just smiled. The one teacher who was the exception to the rule of pleasant behavior gave an introductory, hour-long lecture on French politics at the usual speed of light. I comprehended virtually nothing, although at the end of the lecture I could tell where one word ended and another began. Real progress. Then, she gave a pop quiz, which seemed to be an analysis of a political cartoon. After fifteen minutes I deciphered the cartoon, but had no idea why it was funny. It certainly wasn't funny to *me*. I waited after class and confessed. She looked down her nose at me and said in French, "If you don't know the language, what are you doing here?"

Good question, I thought.

The good news about school is that I was the star of the English class. Don't laugh. It's something. And after they became accustomed to my daily presence, some of the kids actually spoke to me. They seemed genuinely glad to meet an American. This did not extend to their social life. The kids were pleasant at school, but they didn't invite me over to their homes. One reason is that the students at the lycée don't all live in Valence. Many came in on the bus, just as I did, from the surrounding towns and villages. Nobody drives a car. It is unusual, even for the French kids, to socialize after school, and even to do so on the weekends, unless you live in the same village, requires serious advance planning and one or more bus rides. I'm accustomed to going out both Friday and Saturday nights with my friends in Connecticut. These kids are lucky if they go out once or twice a month!

One day, however, two of my classmates invited me to take a walking tour of Valence after our Saturday morning class. The sky was a brilliant, cloudless blue. There were flowers everywhere, and palm trees in the center of town. We toured the old city, which has narrow, winding cobblestone streets, and visited the Cathedral of St. Appollinaire, which was completed in 1095. The town I live in in Connecticut was established in 1708 and was actually the scene of a Revolutionary War battle in 1777. I thought that was pretty impressive, but this church is nine hundred years old and it's *big*. Nearby, in the town of Orange, there are also Roman ruins, which are two thousand years old. Time and human history become vividly real when you can touch the things made by human hands so long ago.

After our tour of Valence we sat on a bench beside the Rhône river, and we talked. My classmates forgot about my "disability" and talked at their normal lightning speed. I followed the general meaning of the entire conversation, and I found that when I relaxed I could also make myself understood, haltingly, but entirely in French. It was a very good day.

That evening at dinner I was full of my social success, and I made a real effort to contribute to the conversation. I did pretty well until we were ready for the dessert course, which was yogurt with my host Mom's homemade peach "confiture." I offered to help assemble and serve the dessert, and attempted to ask, "Should I put the preserves in the yogurt?" I tried the word "*préservatifs*" for preserves. There was silence at the table, and then hysterical laughter. Finally, they recovered enough to tell me that "*préservatif*" means condom in French.

THREE

Je Mange

(I EAT)

Valence is a great place to live if you love food. It's a market town on the Rhône river between Lyon and Avignon. Once a Roman colony, people have been living there since 43 B.C. And if my experience is any indicator, they came for the food. In Valence, eating well is taken for granted. The reason is easy to see. Fruits, vegetables, and herbs for the whole country are produced there, in addition to crusty bread, croissants, sweet butter, thick jam, honey, wheels of creamy cheese, olives, sweet melons from Cavaillon, peaches, and pears, even kiwi fruit, mangoes, and figs. Not to mention wine. More later on that subject.

My host family upheld the traditions of the region. Lunch is the big meal of the day and school closes down from noon to 2:00 P.M. so that students and teachers can go home and eat a proper meal. They would consider our school lunches of bagels and cream cheese, chicken nuggets, hamburgers, or pizza uncivilized. The very idea of fast food, not to mention fast food itself, is looked down on by most of the French people I have met.

Almost everything the family ate was purchased fresh from the market that day. That isn't to say the French prepare everything from scratch on a daily basis. In fact many people buy and serve prepared foods frequently. Some typical take-home foods are meat pies, quiches, marinated vegetables, lasagna, specialty breads, and lemon or nut tarts for dessert. French shoppers go to a *supermarché* for the convenience, but they also visit the *boulangerie* daily for bread. In Valence there were four bakeries, plus *pâtisseries*, *boucheries*, *marchands des fruits* and *légumes* and, of course, *fromageries*. The array of cheeses was mind-boggling and, from an American perspective, frightening. The fat content was often 50–75 percent. There were also stores called *tabac*. They are the *only* places in France one can buy cigarettes, magazines, and newspapers. And there were numerous wine merchants. Before the holidays, my dad suggested that I buy my host family wine for Christmas as a gift from my Connecticut family. He said I could probably find an adult to shop with me and actually make the purchase. Little did he know that absolutely anyone, including sixteen-year-old American girls, can buy wine anywhere in France, and drink it. *Pas grave*. Nobody under eighteen, however, can drive a car legally. The perspective is entirely different.

The French all seemed to have *heard* of cholesterol, low-fat diets, and sugar substitutes, but it was very hard for them to *believe* that any sane person would remove from food all the things that make it taste good—particularly from dairy products. Low-fat or skim milk simply doesn't exist there, and the idea of removing the butterfat from *cheese* is unthinkable. The French have a word for eating and drinking simply because it tastes wonderful: *gourmandise*. Most everything tastes great, but some cultural differences take a little getting used to. The milk (4 percent butterfat) does not require refrigeration. It can sit on the shelf for months. At first it was all I could do to bring myself to taste it. I must not have been subtle because my family explained at length that French milk is not only pasteurized; it is sterilized. Since it has no bacteria, it can't go sour. *Je comprends*, but it's still warm milk.

Raw meat was even more unsettling. My host ordered that in Paris. I was minding my own business at the salad bar and when I returned to the table, there it was: a plate full of raw hamburger with a *raw egg and two small flat fish* on the top. I prayed no one would ask me to try it because my mother said I should try everything I was offered at least once. Sorry, Mom. The French also have a taste for parts of animals, and even whole animals Americans don't often eat, like brains, thymus glands and tripe, feet, frog's legs, and bunny rabbits. My first trip to the *supermarché* was an education in itself. Small corpses were hanging from the ceiling where we would buy meat in plastic packages. Some of the little beasts were decapitated and skinned, but others were furry and complete. From the French perspective this is a good thing, because one knows precisely what one is getting and that the animal is freshly killed. All I know is that I have never knowingly eaten a bunny rabbit, and the chances that I ever will now are extremely remote. This is also the land of the truffle and truffle worship. They are a great delicacy and too expensive even for most French families. Occasionally one can see whole truffles in a specialty store. They look like giant black mushrooms with warts, but they are rumored to taste heavenly. I haven't had the pleasure. I have, however, tasted chestnuts: boiled, fried, baked, roasted over charcoal. Any style is fine with me. Chestnuts are sublime.

As Thanksgiving approached far away in Connecticut, I found myself daydreaming about traditional American foods that don't exist in Valence. I thought about peanut butter, bagels, and salsa with tortilla chips *all the time,* but in November I began remembering holiday foods especially. Thanksgiving has always been a favorite holiday of mine, because the whole family gathers together to eat my favorite meal of the year, and eat and eat some more. I never gave much thought to the actual preparation of the meal, although I was aware that my mother slaved in the kitchen for weeks, preparing breads, plum puddings, assorted pies, brandy hard sauce, cranberry sauce, relishes, and preserves (no *préservatifs*). I wasn't prepared, however, for the curiosity about the holiday which the French expressed. How could one meal assume such significance, they wondered?

You have to understand that what *wasn't* said by the French was actually more than what *was* said. The question really meant, what *American* meal could be worth so much effort?

There was some genuine interest in the history of the holiday, combined with an even more genuine disdain for American food. The question also meant, "You came here to learn the French language and culture. Our cuisine, our food, is, quite simply, the best in the world. It is a great part of our culture. Why are you rattling on incessantly about *dindes* (turkeys)?" I explained about the Pilgrims and the Indians, about how they sat down together and shared their food, giving thanks for the first harvest in the New World, and how the Indians brought a *dinde* to the feast. And now all Americans of all religions and ethnic backgrounds in fifty states, some of them separated by great oceans, sit down on the same day and eat the same meal and give thanks that they are Americans. Tears of patriotism welled up in my eyes. The French averted their eyes. Displays of emotion, except over dogs, are in poor taste.

But I was not to be deterred. I would have Thanksgiving dinner if I had to cook it myself. If only I had listened to the little voice which said, "No, no, not that." There is something about being a minority in a faraway place that gives you the determination to stand up and be recognized, however unwise. I knew my fellow American, Megan-from-Maine, whom the French called Megan-la-grande to distinguish her from me, Megan-la-petite, was experiencing similar nostalgia and determination. (A word of explanation is necessary here. The French are small people. Megan-la-grande means Megan-the-tall. She is 5'9", and she towered above most Frenchmen we knew. For a whole year this perfectly normal

American girl felt like a giant. Since we both lived in the same small town, attended the same lycée, and were close friends, the French families who knew us took to calling us Megan-la-grande and Megan-la-petite. At 5'6", I am not petite, but everything is relative, even in France. Eventually our identical names were dropped and we became simply La-grande and La-petite.)

La-grande and I discussed the problem and agreed that we would just have to pool our resources and create an American Thanksgiving in France. I had never planned or cooked any part of the Thanksgiving feast before. Actually it was worse than that. My entire culinary *répertoire* at the time consisted of waffles, omelets, oatmeal cookies, and one quiche. It was a very good quiche, I might add, but the only one I ever made. My co-chef was equally accomplished. But almost three months in France taught us both not to let our obvious short-comings deter us from trying anything. Admittedly our joint inexperience presented a problem, but it was only a turkey after all. Compared to the daily horror of physics in French, this would be *pas grave* for sure. In our crazed minds the hard-est part of making Thanksgiving happen was not preparing the food, but finding a French family that was willing to sacri-fice just one of their 365 fine French dinners in order to eat American food. In their minds the American diet consists of le Big Macs, fries, and sugar-coated cereals, washed down by Coke or "Bud." I should take a moment right here to mention that this is all part of an important French schizophrenia about

America. They are secretly impressed by our dominance as a world power, even intimidated. They also think we are unworthy of such dominance because we aren't, well, we're not French. This attitude leads to some interesting behavior. The French will put down everything American—language, culture (or lack of it), food, clothes, films, you name it. At the very same time, they are speaking Franglais (*le weekend, le rock and roll*), standing in line to eat Chicago-style pizza, le Big Mac, and Tex-Mex taco plates, and wearing Levi's while they watch American movies, dubbed in French. In school I was actually subjected to "educational" films about our outrageous eating habits which stated that virtually everyone in America is overweight and unhealthy. I was expected to participate in the discussions which followed this propaganda.

Knowing all this, I was even more determined to treat my French hosts to one exceptional American dinner. Pride goeth before a fall.

Eventually, La-grande wore down her host family, the Rollets, and they wearily agreed to lend us their kitchen so that we could prepare an American Thanksgiving. Her American mom sent the French family a children's book about Thanksgiving, to acquaint them with the historical background for the holiday and the traditional foods. Along with the book she included cranberries and a recipe for cranberry sauce. We were on our way. My mom sent the crucial recipes for stuffings, breads, pies, and the *pièce de résistance* at our house, brandy hard sauce. We decided to forget the plum pudding.

Even if we could make one, and we couldn't, we decided plum pudding is overrated. What was essential was the hard sauce. Plum pudding is just an excuse to eat hard sauce anyway.

What did present a problem, however, was the absence of certain foods which are absolutely necessary to any self-respecting Thanksgiving feast. The produce for this entire country is grown in the Rhône river valley, and distributed from Valence, but do you think you can find a sweet potato or even an acorn squash? Marshmallows were a problem, too, although in the absence of sweet potatoes, marshmallows didn't really matter. The beast itself was a bit of a concern, though. (As it turned out, the turkey was a serious problem, but that became evident only later.) Turkeys do exist in southern France, but they must be only distant cousins of American turkeys. I hesitate to use the word scrawny, because that sounds like I'm putting them down. French turkeys are slender. All in all, the meal presented an interesting challenge. We just hoped the kind French family who volunteered to eat it wouldn't feel equally challenged. In my opinion, if they could eat *steak tartare* and Easter bunnies, they could choke down one thin turkey. At the last minute we decided to buy some wine, though, to distract them from the food. And we knew the pumpkin pies would be good because somebody else made them for us. The French do grow and eat pumpkins.

In fact, they make delicious pumpkin soup. Pumpkin pie, however, doesn't excite them as a concept.

Finally D-Day arrived, meaning *Dinde*-Day. The name was more well chosen than I knew. I saw La-grande after second period; we hugged and she gobbled a few times, eliciting a few questioning stares from our classmates, who had, of course, forgotten that this ordinary Thursday in November was in fact a day of great significance to us. When I think back on my year in France a handful of moments stand out, like still frames. This is one. La-grande gobbled. My classmates stared. Time stopped. Suddenly I realized how far away from home I really was. When I recovered, I gobbled back, a little too loudly, and marched down the hall, head held high.

When school was over, I went home to gather my recipes and the bread for my mother's famous spinach stuffing. I had requested a loaf of white bread, but received a bag of strange, oversize croutons, probably intended for hors d'oeuvres. *Pas grave*, I thought. I can handle this. It was 2:30 P.M. when I arrived at La-grande's house. Dinner was scheduled for 8:30 P.M., meaning we'd have to work fast. I prepared the stuffing and waited for Madame Rollet, La-grande's host mother, to return with the turkey. It is here that the nightmare began.

I'll never know exactly what happened at the *supermarché*. All I know is that what Mrs. Rollet returned with was no ordinary-looking bird. In fact, it was no bird at all. Apparently she was unimpressed with the *dindes*, so she bought a deer! Bambi for Thanksgiving dinner. An outrage. When I saw it, I wanted to die. It was a very large gray-blue slab with no fixed shape. My mouth hung open. I wanted to scream. But clearly she was proud of her purchase, and I couldn't think of an appropriate French insult on such short notice, anyway. I just stood there with my stuffing bowl in my arms, staring at the thing on the counter and wondering how one stuffed a deer slab. I had a violent fantasy in which I shoved the picture book with a big turkey on the cover into Mrs. Rollet's face and asked her if she was crazy or what? TURKEY, *s'il vous plait*, D-I-N-D-E; not DEER, D-A-I-M. It occurred to me that she might be deaf. I took a deep breath and looked around for a roasting pan big enough for this beast, which I decided I would place on top of the stuffing, and hope for the best.

Even this was not to be. I walked toward the place where the oven was—where it had been only a few days earlier. In its place was a large hole in the wall with a jumble of black electrical cords hanging out like dead garden snakes. At first I couldn't react. I stood frozen, stuffing bowl clutched to my body, trying to make sense of what I saw. Then I turned slowly to La-grande. "Oh, yeah," she mumbled under her breath. "The oven broke two days ago. It hasn't been replaced yet." I still held on to a tiny glimmer of hope that this was all a joke, and the new oven would materialize in another location. But in my heart I knew this was some sick version of reality, and I was stuck with it. I figured it explained why Bambi was going to grace our Thanksgiving table. We could spread the deer with cranberry sauce, which Meg had made in advance. But how was I to bake the stuffing, the potatoes, the popovers, the broccoli soufflé? My eyes roved the kitchen in desperation. I focused on my last hope—the microwave.

But how to use the microwave and two gas burners to prepare an entire Thanksgiving dinner? The answer was across the sea in a small New England town. I called Mom.

My mom hadn't cooked any deer lately either, but she suggested I try cooking the stuffing separately in the microwave. She found a microwave cookbook and read me the instructions. Then she suggested I try braising the deer in a big skillet with a cover for about a half hour per pound. She didn't know anything about kilos. Madame Rollet must have made the same decision while I was on the phone because when I returned to the kitchen with my notes, the thing was sizzling away in olive oil with onions and garlic. What could be more American? We handed out the French wine and French cheese and went to work on the side dishes with heavy hearts.

It got worse.

The Rollets had invited another French family and their small children, undoubtedly in a gesture of goodwill. They all waited patiently while we did what we could in the kitchen. Eventually, the stuffing was done. At least the microwave had done what it could. The result was a white mass about the consistency of cold oatmeal, and equally appealing. Perfect with blue meat, I thought. The only time La-grande and I spoke to each other was when we fought over who would have to carry the stuffing into the dining room. I lost. La-grande carried her cranberry sauce in and passed it around to the guests. I took advantage of the distraction to bring in the mess that might have been stuffing, but wasn't. I placed the dish at one end of the table and distanced myself from it as much as I could. Actually, the braised venison was pretty good, and the mashed potatoes were fine, but mashed potatoes are common in France. Mrs. Rollet sneaked in a regional side dish of chestnuts. And there was plenty of good French bread.

I could tell you that La-grande and I rose to the occasion, that the French families were witty and delightful, that the feast, while not American, was enjoyed by all. I could tell you that, but I would be lying. The French raised their glasses of good French wine in a toast to America, and then fell silent. Conversation was as plentiful as the turkey, or as absent as the oven, whichever you prefer. Mr. Rollet, who seemed otherwise to be a nice person, spoke only to question our intelligence. He was quite certain that Thanksgiving fell on the third Thursday in November; not the fourth. Having spoken to my mother only a few hours earlier and knowing she was preparing her *dinde* for the oven at that time, I was having none of that. Not altogether graciously, I asked Mr. Rollet what his source was for this misinformation. Well, it was his English teacher, of course. And what nationality was his English teacher? Irish! Not Irish-American; his English teacher was from Ireland. After that exchange, the silence deepened. Not only could we not prepare edible American food; we were a social disaster. The longer the silence continued, the more painful it became. I was aware of a sound in the background, penetrating the silence at regular intervals. In my mind it got louder and louder, until I finally looked around for the source. It was the grandfather clock, ticking away. I had been in the house a dozen times before and never once heard it tick.

And then, at last, someone spoke! I couldn't understand the words, but the sounds were human and coming from the four-year-old girl seated next to me. I turned to respond, and the wave of relief which had started to wash over me was replaced by horror. The child was blue. I thought, irrelevantly, that her face was exactly the color of raw deer meat. Then it was clear. She was choking. I hit her on the back. Her mother started screaming. Her father leapt into action, picked her up, hung her upside down, slapping her back. The chestnut that was wedged in her throat shot out across the table.

All I could think of was how thankful I was that it was French food that nearly killed her. This absurd thought struck me as incredibly funny. I knew if I looked at La-grande, I would start laughing, and that if I started laughing, I wouldn't be able to stop, and that if that happened, it would be so great a *faux pas* that I would be banished from all decent French homes in Valence. My shoulders shook, and I snorted, but I managed to refrain from real laughter. Fortunately, the afflicted family decided to leave immediately, before the cheese and dessert courses, and in the confusion, nobody noticed my strange behavior.

And then the phone rang. It was my family, calling from Connecticut to share with me the blessings of the day. Mom, Dad, sister, brother, brother-in-law, baby niece, and our neighbors, the Martins, were all together sipping California champagne, while the great *dinde* roasted to a deep golden brown, and thinking of me. How was *my* feast, they asked? I could hear laughter in the background and in my mind I smelled the juicy turkey far away across the Atlantic Ocean. "Different", I said.

They wouldn't have believed the truth.

FOUR

Je Comprends
(I UNDERSTAND)

When it happened, I was sitting in the café Victor Hugo in Valence. The waiter had just brought me a glass of hot cocoa, thick and rich as cream. As I stirred the chocolate with the cinnamon stick provided for that purpose, I listened to the buzz of conversations all around me. Christmas carols were playing in the background, and two old men had taken the table next to mine. As I watched them, they unrolled a traveling chessboard and opened a bag of wooden pieces. Outside the café young people walked by wearing heavy woolen sweaters and the long scarves in fashion with both sexes. The bitter wind called the mistral caught the scarves and sent them twisting in the air. The temperature doesn't drop much below freezing in Valence, but the wind makes it feel much colder, and no one outdoors was stopping to chat.

On that particular day in early December I had only two classes and hours of free time between them. Like other French students, I came to the café to study. In France you can order one drink and stay as long as you please. It is the custom, and no one hurries you to move on. I had been there perhaps a dozen times in the three and a half months I had lived in France, but this visit was different. As I listened, one old man spoke to the other, and, lining up the chess pieces slowly with a gnarled hand, the other man responded. Suddenly, with no warning, I realized I understood *every word* they were saying. More than that, I understood everything else that was being said all around me. I wasn't straining to catch the meaning; my heart rate wasn't elevated; my palms weren't sweaty. I was no longer an anxious outsider looking in at an alien culture. I was part of the scene.

One hundred days and a lifetime had passed since I stepped off the Bullet Train from Paris, alone and homesick and terrified. One hundred days had passed, and I had conquered the French language. Well, OK, maybe not *conquered*, but I was competent, and getting better every day. Something powerful happened that day at the café Victor Hugo which is hard to put into words in any language, and as a result I became a different person. France became my home on that day, for a time, and I was at home there. I had made French friends, both male and female. I had made English-speaking AFS friends from all over the world—Maine to New Zealand. I had gone places and done things I had never even dreamed of a year earlier.

At the same time, in the classroom, I began to understand my teachers, and every once in a while I could actually raise my hand with the right answer in French as fast as my native-speaking classmates. I had not conquered the lycée Emile Loubet yet, but I began to believe it was possible, just possible, to do well in honors classes taught in a foreign language. No drug could produce the natural high I felt at that moment. I know I gasped when the realization hit me, because the old men turned and stared at me. Normally that behavior would make me uncomfortable, but right then I didn't care at all. I wanted to walk over to their table and shake them both and tell them, "I understand!" *Je comprends!* But that probably would've gotten me arrested. So I settled for smelling the cocoa and the cinnamon, and listening. I listened for two hours, filled with elation.

The only comparison I can think of doesn't do the moment justice, but it's all I have. When I was in ninth grade I went to Belize, in Central America, with my family. We went because we are SCUBA divers, and Belize has a barrier reef famous among divers. We took just one night dive, but it will stay with me forever. We fell backwards off the dive boat into darkness and silence, and then suddenly the deep was illuminated by the dive captain's giant flashlight. What had been darkness became a riot of light and color and movement. The coral reef was before me in pink and blue and yellow, and the warm seas were thick with neon-colored fish. I forgot to breathe for a moment. I had fallen from outer space into an alien environment of unimaginable beauty. For over three months, the French language was like the barrier reef: beautiful, alien, and seemingly impenetrable but suddenly penetrated. Then, like that flash of light under the sea that revealed another universe, suddenly I became part of something new. And after that, everything changed.

As Christmas and the New Year approached *à grande vitesse,* I began to think for the first time about all I had learned in the past few months and all I had to be grateful for. Obviously, I was becoming proficient in a second language—something few high-school students ever have the opportunity to do. You can't master a foreign language in the classroom. You have to *be there*, and being there is painful. Sometimes it hurts too much for words. Some kids give up and go home. I don't blame them. No one can prepare you for the isolation, the sense of being profoundly *different*. No one can prepare you for the way you feel when someone laughs at your early efforts to communicate. No one can prepare you for the loss of all your lifelines in one day. One day you have Mom and Dad, brother and sister and dog and a network of loving friends, supportive teachers, and parents of friends. The next day they are all gone.

But it gets better. You reach within yourself for strength because there's nowhere else to reach, and you find a little something. You become acutely aware of your surroundings, perhaps because you have no one to talk to, and the brain needs to keep busy. As it happened, my surroundings were beautiful. The town of Valence was unremarkable, but the region it is in, called Ardêche, is one of stark contrasts and harsh beauty. From my bedroom window I looked out on a white stone cliff named Mount Crussol, which has a ruined château at the top. The view never failed to take my breath away. There are tiny triumphs, too small to mention, really, but they make a difference. And you slowly begin to adapt. Words begin to have meaning. People begin to make friendly overtures. You are actually invited to a social event. Teens don't socialize as much in France, but when they do, they make up for lost time. The French seem to be doting parents. Teenagers don't drive, so the parents drive the kids to a discothèque and return to pick them up when it closes, at 4 A.M! My mom will do a lot for me, but that one is out of the question. Not in this lifetime.

Evenings were hardest at first. The phone never rang. I had almost no friends, but even if I had had thousands, French teens don't talk on the phone just to pass the time or to compare notes on the day at school. Telephone withdrawal was enough all by itself to send me into an emotional tailspin. So my host family advised me to join some groups which have evening meetings. I joined an art class and a rock-climbing club. None of my classmates were in these groups, but I met people, and I got out. In the evenings we climbed an artificial indoor wall, but before long we were out hanging off cliffs, and I felt joy and exhilaration. In my art class people complimented my work, and my confidence began to return.

The organization of the French school year helped me a lot, too. French high-school students go to school for about two months, followed by a two-week vacation. This continues throughout the school year. The last break is at the end of May, and it is followed at the end of June with a two-month holiday. The whole country shuts down in July and August, and it was at the end of that *vacance* that I appeared on the scene. That is why I thought the French people did nothing but party, drink wine, and sit around talking at outdoor cafés. The truth was they were storing up the good times while they could. School was about to start, and after that fun was going to be in short supply. I was like one of the blind men feeling the elephant; I only understood a small part of the whole story.

And that is what happened at the café Victor Hugo that afternoon in early December. I had learned to speak French, but more than that, I learned to understand and respect a foreign culture and people. I am far richer for the experience.

FIVE

Je me Souviens

(I REMEMBER)

On the day in early February that I completed half of my stay in France, there was a hint of spring in Rhône river valley. The high Alps, where I would soon be skiing, were still buried under a heavy blanket of snow, but in Valence the weather had become changeable: soft rain and warm temperatures one day, light snow and bitter wind the next. More like mid-March in Connecticut, except that here in the Ardêche some of the flowers bloom year-round and the snow, when it comes, melts quickly. By February I was actually beginning to wonder if there was enough time left to do everything I wanted to do and go everywhere I wanted to go. I also made a new beginning in February by moving for the second half of my year in France to the home of a new host family. As I packed up my duffel bag, I found the calendar my mother had sent with me stuck under a pile of books and papers. I had quite forgotten about it, but as I picked it up, memories flooded back and my eyes stung. I flipped back to

September, with its photo of a park in Paris, brilliant with yellow leaves under a bright blue sky. My first thought was that I have yet to see Paris when the sky was blue and cloudless. But then I looked down at the calendar and my chest hurt with the power of remembrance. I remember thinking that if I had to repeat those first thirty to forty-five days in order to get to this place, I could not. (But now, looking back on the whole experience from the safety of my home in Connecticut, I believe I would choose to do it again.)

In the beginning I crossed off the days on my calendar, one, by one, by one—a procession of little white boxes stretching ahead without end. It was a kind of ritual. The crossed lines in the boxes are dark and heavy. I was pressing hard with the pencil. At first they are neatly within the squares, but after a few weeks they become slashes, through the boxes and out into the white spaces. Some boxes are heavily circled. Two are blacked out completely. Dark days. I don't remember now what it was I wanted to forget.

There are no words on the calendar. I didn't need to write on it because I kept track of my schedule in an appointment book, and I had a travel diary so I'd remember place names and events as I moved around. I also had a ledger, where I recorded the details of daily life and ideas for a column called "Postcards from France" that I tried to send back to my hometown newspaper about once a month.

But the calendar didn't need any words. Looking at it at that point, five months into my journey, it spoke loud and clear. In

the beginning of my stay in France I was inhibited and frus-
trated and angry. I wanted to break through the barriers of language and culture. I wanted to be out in the discos, partying
away with forty or fifty of my new French friends. Who am I
kidding? I would've settled for an hour on a park bench with
one new French friend. My mother used to wonder out loud
(for our benefit) why God didn't see fit to give her just one
child out of three whose greatest joy was to go to school and
learn, just one who spent his or her spare time reading books
or solving mathematical equations. Instead she got three kids
who look at high school as a four-year social event and math as
something you use to figure out the shortest distance
between two parties. But Mom may have found the answer.
Ship us off to France for a year. There is no Homecoming at
lycée Emile Loubet, no Junior Prom, no Spirit Day, no foot-
ball team. What you do get at Loubet is a good, no-nonsense
secondary education. It's a question of priorities and culture.

What caught my attention on the calendar, though, was not
the rows of days I crossed out, but the two days in a row I *forgot* to cross out. When the marks picked up again, they were
lighter, and the pattern shifted gradually. More days were forgotten, two weeks of vacation had an airy, wavy, horizontal
line going through them, and in early December I stopped
keeping a record at all. That is about the time I made my
"breakthrough" with the French language. One day I couldn't
understand; the next day I could, or so it seemed at the time.
One day I thought in English and translated my thoughts

into French, and the next day I thought in French and spoke in French. One night I dreamed in English that I was chasing a train that left me behind at the station in Valence. All my friends from Ridgefield were on the train, and I was calling to them, but they couldn't hear me or couldn't understand what I was saying. The next time I dreamed I was on a train, I told off everyone on it in very passable, if not *gentil* French. I don't know *why* I told them off, but I remember it felt very good, and I was sure they deserved it. I was sure the whole country deserved it.

At first I couldn't remember why I forgot to cross off those two days, but when I looked at my appointment book, it all came back. An acquaintance of mine at the lycée, named Colin, invited me to his house for the afternoon on a Saturday in early October. Colin had spent the previous year at a high school in Oregon, and he was delighted to find a new classmate in Valence who spoke American English. As I mentioned, it's unusual for French teenagers to socialize on Saturdays because they attend school in the morning and are expected to study in the afternoon. So Colin and his family made an extraordinary effort on my behalf. I had a great day. I took the bus to his town. I met Colin's parents and his circle of friends. French teens have tight cliques, and acceptance of a foreigner is neither quick nor easy. By accepting me himself, Colin broke the ice. Later, we took a drive and visited two tiny medieval towns, with roads so narrow you could almost reach out and touch the stone buildings on either side. I got home tired and late and fell asleep without marking my calendar.

The very next day my aunt and uncle from Chicago took a four-hundred-mile detour from Paris just to spend time with me and see my new surroundings. They had a little rental car, and I was proud to be able to lead them right back to the picture-postcard villages I'd discovered the day before, almost like I knew what I was doing. We ate a four-course lunch together and spent the whole day exploring the region, ending up at my new home for dessert and conversation. When I heard they were coming, I was afraid I'd throw myself on the ground and cling to their legs when they tried to leave. And it did cross my mind. But in the end they left, I stayed, and I fell asleep without marking my calendar.

And not long afterward I discovered I had classmates only a two-minute walk from my house. They began to drop over and to invite me to their houses and include me in their social life. At last I *needed* a social calendar! The month of December is just a blur. I spent the holidays in England with my host family. I saw London. It was foreign, but wonderfully familiar, too. The French don't celebrate Christmas with the same gusto and conviction that we do in America. I didn't miss the blaring TV commercials, the plastic poinsettias, or the old men in fake Santa suits with cotton beards, scaring the little children in the mall. There were some things about Christmas in America that I did miss, however. I missed the tiny white lights up and down Main Street, the outdoor decorations all over town, the giant Christmas tree in Rockefeller Center, fragrant cookies, and my old knit Christmas stocking. I missed the glitz, the traditions, and of course, the parties. In France, Christmas is a lot more subtle.

So London came as an excellent surprise, when I shouldn't have been surprised at all. Many of our American traditions do come from England, after all. London was decorated for the holidays in balsam and ribbons and colored lights, and I felt right at home. I had as my personal tour guide a friend of my host family named Kit, whose summer job is tour guiding in London, so I saw it all, and she took the time to make the history come alive. From there I went to the ancient university towns of Oxford and Cambridge, lit up like fairy-tale cities. There I was hosted by Ben, who teaches English in Valence, but whose family lives in Cambridge. I was really only an acquaintance, but Ben drove far out of his way to pick me up, give me the grand tour, and take me home to dinner with his family. Finally I went down to the south of England for Christmas. Throughout England, my hosts treated me like visiting royalty. There is no substitute for Christmas in Connecticut, but if you have to spend Christmas away from home, I recommend England and the English. The only thing I don't recommend, in retrospect, is calling home on Christmas Day. I had spent a lovely morning. The weather was fine, and I had gone for a run in a forest near the sea. The woods were dark and tranquil—a welcome change from the bright lights and bustle of London.

No one was with me, so when I heard a heavy thumping noise, it startled me, and I stopped to look and listen. In front of me in the shadows was a herd of wild horses, chomping and stomping and swishing their long tails. I had nearly run into them. I held my breath and stared. Their eyes were on me, too, but they never stopped eating. Finally I backed slowly away, lost in the wonder of the moment and wondering what to do if I started a stampede. It reminded me of the Christmas morning in Connecticut ten years earlier when my brother looked up from his bowl of Cheerios to see the biggest buck that ever was, standing in the rock garden staring back at him. Tim was smart enough not to move. He just whispered, "Look, look!" and we all did. The buck could hardly lift his great head for the weight of his antlers, and he stood there for a long moment like the horses, watching us watch him, before he walked slowly into the forest. Tim *knew* it was a reindeer getting a late start home to the North Pole, and my parents never told him otherwise. Remembering Connecticut was the problem. Instead of concentrating on the present moment, I wandered back into the past, and I wanted to go back in the worst way. When I called home, my family was just opening the handmade presents I'd sent from France. My grandparents were visiting for the holidays. We are very close. I call my grandfather *Papa*. When he came to the phone and heard my voice, there was a catch in his voice that I felt like a physical pain from across the sea. I don't know if you can't go home again, but I do know you can't call home on Christmas Day when you're sixteen years old and thousands of miles away.

A few days later we flew back from London to Lyon, France. That is the first time I remember thinking of France as *home*. I wanted to be in Valence in time to spend New Year's Eve with dozens or hundreds of my new French friends. Well, maybe not quite that many, but it was a big party, and it was fun to celebrate the beginning of the year *mille neuf cent quatre-vingt quinze* six hours before my friends and family did in Connecticut. Mom was a bit troubled when she heard the unmistakable sound of champagne corks popping so far away, but I reminded her that it was *comme il faut*, and besides, none of us was driving anywhere. French teens may drink wine with dinner frequently and almost everyone smokes, but almost no one drinks and drives.

With my year in France half-over, I had reached the point where I wanted to slow down the clock, at least some of the time, and savor every day, like the French savor fine wines and weird *pâtés*. I was too busy trying to figure out how to take advantage of all the travel and social opportunities in the next five months to waste my time making Xs on a calendar. In February we had a two-week *vacance*, which I spent skiing in the French Alps with four of my French classmates, two of whom, Leane and Marie, had become real friends, the kind one might hope to keep for a lifetime. I hadn't realized until I had no friends at all how important they were to my emotional well-being. Along with many other moments of self-realization, I came to understand in France that I define myself, at least in part, through my relationships with my friends.

So when Leane and Marie proposed that I join their group for a week of skiing near Mont Blanc, I was ecstatic. As it happens, I love to ski, but even if I'd never been on skis in my life, I would've pretended I could ski and taken my chances on an early death in *les hautes Alpes*. This invitation was pretty important to me. Actually, Mont Blanc, at seventeen thousand feet, is the highest of the *vrai* or true Alps, which remain snowcapped throughout the summer. The *hautes* or high Alps are real mountains, but not as high as the true Alps. My father loves little tidbits of trivia like that.

We stayed in a ski chalet in a tiny town at the base of Mont Blanc called Châtel. I've skied every winter in Vermont since I was seven years old, and once I went to the Colorado Rocky Mountains for a week, but no ski experience in my country could have prepared me for the size of Mont Blanc—or for the snow. It snows in New England, and it snows more in Colorado, but this was snow. It snowed all night every night, silently, heavily. If we got up and out before nine in the morning, our group could be the first to disturb the new powder, making our own trails as we glided in and out of the trees. We alternated between using skis and snow boards, just to keep it interesting. I had boarded only once before I went to Mont Blanc, but I recommend it highly for cheap thrills. Your feet remain stationary, clamped to the snowboard, leaving the rest of your body to do all the work, and you go like hell.

While in Châtel, we stayed in a condo owned by Leane's parents. The unit was small, so with seven kids and all our gear in it, we were tripping all over each other. But with the wide Alpine trails literally across the road, we had few complaints. In fact, we had no complaints whatsoever. That week was the one brief period of complete freedom from the stress of school, parents, and studies that we had all year. In France, teenagers spend much of their free time on weekends with their parents, and they study compulsively day and night. But when they let loose, they don't do it halfway. For seven whole days and nights we didn't do anything we didn't want to do, and what we did, we did with abandon. We skied until our legs were weak, then went home and prepared our own meals, to use the word loosely. Nutrition was not an issue. That was one of the restraints we abandoned, along with getting a good night's sleep and studying. We did attempt to be early risers, but after spending most of the night in town, partying strenuously, we weren't always successful. The first one who admitted to being awake in the morning crawled out the door to purchase fresh croissants and bread for *le petit déjeuner*. Fortified, we made our lunches, layered on our ski paraphernalia, and raced each other to the slopes. The ski conditions the first two days were so extraordinary, at least by Vermont standards, that I thought we should skip breakfast and take advantage of the deep powder while we could, but I got nowhere with that suggestion. The looks I got from my friends convinced me to eat my croissants and *ferme la bouche.* What I didn't understand at first was that these conditions in the French Alps were not the exception, but the norm. Day after day we swept over miles of uncharted descents and fields of untouched powder, challenging each other to go farther and faster and seeking our own physical limits. On the third day, after several hours of skiing in the fast lane, I experienced a kind of mind-body exhilaration that was like a drug. I wanted to go out and push my body to the edge again and again, just so I could feel that "high." I am not a runner, but I have heard runners talk about a similar sensation, when you stop feeling tired and suddenly feel you could run forever. It's the mind playing a trick, and you know it, but it doesn't matter. You just want to find that place again and stay there for a while. I want to ski in the Alps again, but I don't think I will return to Châtel again. Maybe it was an effect of the speed, the altitude, and the brilliant white light, or maybe it was just that I was sixteen and absolutely free, but I felt something there I haven't felt before. The French say *l'extase,* but there is no word in English that does the sensation justice.

Fortunately I didn't have long after leaving Mont Blanc to think about paradise lost. No sooner did I return to Valence than I had to pack my duffel again and force myself to go to Paris to meet my grandmother and my Aunt Mary and act as their personal tour guide. In that way February was gone almost before it began and in March my *escalade* group would begin climbing outdoors again and a local skiing group would continue its weekend trips to the Alps and the Massif Central. Then in April, the schools closed again for another two weeks—this *vacance* thoughtfully included my seventeenth birthday.

It was during that time that I met the AFS student who is going to live with me in Connecticut next year. Carole and her parents, Mme. and M. Bagnoud, drove to Valence from Switzerland so we could meet and get to know each other. Opportunities like this occur infrequently among foreign exchange students. I didn't find out who my host family was until the month I was scheduled to leave—August—and then it turned out to be a nontraditional family consisting of a grandmother and her twelve-year-old grandson. Much later, I discovered that I was virtually unplaceable because I requested a nonsmoking family. How was I to know that is a noncompute? Madame Halgrain's might have been the only nonsmoking household in France. Live and learn. In contrast, Carole was placed with us in March. She didn't ask for a nonsmoking household, but, lucky girl, that's what she got. When my mother received the paperwork on Carole, she got out her maps and discovered that the Bagnouds lived close to Lake Geneva, in the southwest corner of Switzerland. *Voilà*, and *pas grave*, she arranged it easily. All that lay between us were the Alps. My mother, who is not known for her map-reading skills, computed the distance, not the terrain. What are a few mountains among friends? As it turned out, the Bagnouds were up for the journey, and we spent two days together exploring the deep gorges and caves of the Ardêche region, which is just south of Valence. Carole and I talked nonstop. It wasn't until she left and my mother asked about her English that I realized we had spoken exclusively in French. By April I was so comfortable with the French language that it never occurred to me to switch to English.

In May there was a minivacation to hold us until school closed in the last week of June. As I looked at this calendar I couldn't imagine why anyone who was lucky enough to be going to high school in France would want to exchange this vacation schedule for the endless school year in Connecticut.

I packed my calendar away in my overstuffed duffel, looked out my bedroom window at Mount Crussol one last time, and moved on.

SIX

Je Rêve

(I DREAM)

My *dad asked me in a letter* if I'd ever thought about, "the American Dream" (I had not), and if there was a corresponding "French Dream" (I had no idea). But the question made me think about American high-school students and their French counterparts. In what ways are we the same, and how are we different? Do the French have a national dream, and if so, what is it? And what about French teenagers? What do they dream of doing or becoming? Then, coincidentally, my English teacher brought up the subject of Marilyn Monroe and, what else, the American Dream. It was then that I knew I would have to stop dreaming about exotic travel destinations long enough to tackle the much more difficult subject of the two different cultures and high schools I had experienced.

In a way, I was living the American Dream while I lived in France. When I was a sophomore I decided I wanted to try what AFS had to offer—total immersion in a foreign language and culture for one year: a new family, friends, school, future. My teachers, friends, parents, counselors—everyone warned me of the potholes I could fall in that would make it harder to get in the college of my choice. For the "top" colleges it wouldn't be good enough just to go there and become bilingual; I would be expected to go there, become bilingual, and get good grades in classes taught entirely in a foreign language. (Now that I see that in writing, I realize I must have been quite *folle* at the time to pursue the idea after hearing that.) But some people said, "If this is really what you want, go for it. Take the risk. What you will gain in the end is far greater than what you may lose, short-term."

They could say that because in America the future is still wide-open for people who know what they want and are willing to work hard to get it. And in America there isn't just one path to success. It can be academics, sports, music, art, theater, or dance—even writing! America values the individual. It's OK for kids in the US to join a rock band, become actors, cartoonists, pilots, mechanics. It's OK to be different, even weird.

It isn't as easy in France.

First, there is no French Dream. I know that because I tried the direct approach. I asked French people. The first person I talked to was my host mom. "*Il n'y a pas de rêve francais*," she said. "*Ça n'existe pas. D'accord?*" ("There is no French dream. It doesn't exist." *D'accord* is used frequently and literally means something closer to OK. But here my host was ending the discussion, whether it was "OK" or not.) The French have a way of making statements like that which are absolute and final. The last word on the subject, so to speak. But I had a writing assignment, so I pressed on. "What do you mean? How can you be so sure?" She answered that, "America was built on dreams. France just is—and always was." I think she meant that France has a recorded history that goes back to the time of Julius Caesar, and beyond. But I still wasn't satisfied.

The next day I asked my friends if French teenagers have a Dream, and if so, what is it? They reminded me that, "School is life and life is school." Right, I responded, but you *must* have a dream. I thought I knew the answer to this one, but I wanted to hear someone *say* it, so I could be sure. "We don't have time to dream," Manu said. "We've got about seven hours of classroom work a day and four hours of homework every night, including Saturdays. It is, of course, too much for young people, *to breathe always the still air of the classroom*. But we must pass our exam. If French students do have a dream, it is to pass the BAC—with a perfect score."

The two tests are not comparable, but that would be roughly equivalent to getting a 1600 on the SATs, or an 800 on every SAT II subject test you took. The BAC, or Baccalaureate exam, tests a French student in every subject area we are familiar with, plus philosophy, which we do not even take in high school. A high score on the BAC, and the future is wide-open. And with few exceptions, the BAC is the *only* path to success. It's a ticket to the university of your choice and a secure job later. That's the goal. The problem, according to my French classmates, is that the system rewards conformity and discourages individualism, turns kids into "*légumes*." They don't mean literally "vegetables," but something more like robots, who don't know how to do anything but study, and are afraid even to get a cold because they may get behind in their studies. And in France the teachers don't come in early or stay after school to help one student catch up. They come in. They lecture. They leave. *C'est tout.*

French teachers motivate students with plain old-fashioned fear. For the record, it works. These kids learn. They get a great education. But that's all they get. Nobody is "well-rounded," or even understands the term. There are no "jocks." If you want to play a sport, it's on your own time and at your own expense. Kids here aren't pushed to excel at anything except academics. Nobody cares about how many years you took piano lessons, dance lessons, played basketball or ice hockey; how many clubs you joined, races you won, elective offices you held. All that is irrelevant. It's very simple. There is one goal. There is one dream. The BAC. The pressure to perform academically is awesome. But there is no pressure to do or be good at anything else at the same time. Is the French secondary-school system better or worse than the American system? I don't know. It sure is different.

SEVEN

Je Souffre
(I SUFFER)

Kids *at lycée Emile Loubet* who don't perform academically have a very hard time. In France you perform, or else. There are no second chances. You don't have the option of throwing out one bad score. And don't even think about arguing over a grade. You get your homework in on time, and it's done correctly. Nobody would dream of "forgetting" to do the homework, or saying *le chien* ate it. Not if they value their lives. Strangely, however, the homework counts for absolutely nothing toward your grade. You must do it, but it doesn't count, and the teacher never corrects it and returns it. At Ridgefield High, homework usually counts for about 20 percent of the grade, and most teachers consider classroom participation when they compute the grade.

Not in France. In fact, classroom participation as I knew it doesn't happen at Loubet. The only time French students raise their hands is to answer a direct question. Students don't volunteer information or express opinions or ask questions. They respond when spoken to. And by the way, kids never talk to each other during the class, send notes, slouch down in their chairs, or even let their eyes wander from the face of the instructor. This is a good thing, except for the eyes. Try staring at your physics teacher nonstop for two hours. Can't be done by Americans. Our eyes have too much practice wandering over to the windows. In the beginning, when I couldn't understand the language, I also did drawings of the teachers. This is really bad. But remember, as far as my brain was concerned, it was receiving strange, unknown, and meaningless sounds. It shut down regularly because of overload. As I began to understand French, I stopped drawing pictures of the more colorful professors and writing clever little descriptions of them to entertain myself.

I saved the cartoon I did of my French teacher, though, because I thought it particularly good and because the day I drew the picture was memorable in any language. My French teacher didn't teach French, of course. He taught French literature and composition, and no one was there to have fun. The professor was short and round and bald. He had a large, red nose, which I attributed to the red Côte de Rhône wine which is served and drunk in abundance in the Ardèche. When the professor got upset, his whole head went scarlet, and his nose deepened to purple. The day I drew his picture was a purple-nose day. This was the class from hell. The day before, the professor had given a writing assignment in class. The students had two hours to brainstorm, outline, write a rough draft and a final copy. The assignment was to write a well-organized essay, with examples from literature, on the quote: "A man who doesn't laugh is not truly human." Nobody was laughing. He collected the papers at the end of the class and had corrected them for the next day's class.

He was furious. For forty minutes he stood in front of the class reading the papers out loud, including the author's name. No insult or degradation was too extreme. One student's essay incensed him so much he waved it around in the air, then threw it to the floor and stomped on it.

It was Mustapha's paper. He was the first French student who wanted to be my friend. He's the one who invited me on a walking tour of Valence after school. I will always like Mustapha. The scene was all the worse for me because he was the one being humiliated. When the class was finally over and the students filed out, that crushed paper was still on the floor. At this point in my stay I wasn't being asked to write literary essays, but I did have a writing assignment. Apparently my efforts were beneath contempt, or he couldn't think of anything horrible enough to describe my writing. I didn't care what the reason was. I was spared. It's a jungle over there.

As you can easily see, the French experience in the classroom is strikingly different from the American experience. American high-school teachers do not often insult, degrade, or terrorize their pupils. American students usually know what our teachers think of our work, but some effort is made to soften the blow when we try but just don't get it right. And American teachers almost never read our work out loud and then announce the grade to the whole world. There is some privacy, and when I return to American classrooms, I'll be more grateful for that than I ever was before. French teachers teach differently and have a different relationship with their students. They prepare a lesson, come to school, and deliver the lesson. The actual instructive part of the process doesn't happen in France the way it happens in America. There isn't any give-and-take. Students here raise their hands only to answer questions.

It is unusual to ask questions and really strange to suggest a different way of looking at a question or an alternate way of solving a problem. The professor in France is sort of like the pope and my dad—infallible. This doesn't exactly encourage creativity. But it does encourage you to work hard and apply yourself. The alternative is to watch *your* paper get ground into the floor. I wouldn't be fair if I didn't say that good efforts are praised and read out loud for the whole world to hear, too.

The French grading system is not letters, but numbers, from 0 to 20. Nobody ever gets a 20. The French are very tough graders. "Average" grades fall between 7 and 14. Below 7 is pretty bad and 15–18 is very good. Even I, who am a native English speaker, did not receive a 20 in English from my teacher, who was not a native English speaker. The teacher learned and taught British English. There are some differences in vocabulary and usage. I caught on pretty quickly. American English, when it is different from British English, is *wrong*. The kids, however, wanted to hear American English, especially slang, which made her really wild. My classmates loved it when I read out loud, and they tried to copy my

Yankee accent. This teacher was an exception to the rule of "Professor as God." She didn't lecture, and the classes were animated and relaxed. The *Première* group is the equivalent of juniors in high school, and students have had six years of pretty intensive instruction in English. Everyone reads and understands basic texts, but they are not fluent speakers.

After five months in the country, my French and that of most of the other AFS kids was better than the English of our French classmates. This might not have been the case if we had lived somewhere other than France. I remember meeting German and Scandinavian high-school kids who spoke almost faultless English, and in Italy I met more than one teenager who spoke three languages, including English, very well. France is different. That realization came to me slowly, mostly because of the language barrier. I had heard and seen news broadcasts from the beginning, but the radio and TV were even more incomprehensible, if possible, than the real live people. Café talk, as I began to comprehend more, was often about politics, but it was about French politics mostly, not world politics. I didn't realize how out of touch I was until I traveled to London at Christmastime. The BBC was everywhere, telling me about world events, including events in America, which don't get much press in France, at least not in Valence. I was also thrilled to walk down the streets of London and Cambridge and pass by restaurants of every ethnic description, from Indian and Italian to Thai and Szechuan—not to mention Chicago-style deep-dish pizza,

American steak joints, and English pub food on every corner. London seemed cosmopolitan. France seemed, well, French. When you get on a plane in New York and drop down out of the sky in France there is no question but that you have entered another reality. You live and breathe, eat and drink, hear and speak French almost exclusively. There is no escape, and in the end that is a good thing.

If one of my friends at Emile Loubet came to Ridgefield High, he or she could get by. The language-shock would not be as profound as mine was. The culture, classroom, and social shock would be severe, though. As students I think they would find us bold and familiar with our teachers, who would seem shockingly friendly, casual, and helpful. Academically, my friends would do very well at RHS, once they became comfortable with the language, because they are accustomed to working hard six days a week. Culturally, they would find us strange in some ways and similar in others. At home in France the children rule. By our standards, the average French child is spoiled. There is almost nothing a French parent won't do for his child, and, in addition, the kids do not work either in or outside the home. Most don't do dishes or mow the lawn or work after school in the pizza parlor or the gas station. On the other hand, the kids are expected to get good grades. French parents do not accept any excuses. The kids don't even try to invent them. School is serious business in France. Socially, the French town I lived in was not unlike Ridgefield, middle-class. The girls form tight little groups of friends and don't even know the names of girls in different groups, even though they've been in the same school for six years or more. The groups don't socialize with each other. Partly this is because there are no sports or extracurricular activities at school where kids might mix with each other according to their interests. There are no jocks, although there are naturally athletic people. There are no bodybuilders among the boys, and the girls are ultrafeminine. They wouldn't recognize a muscle if they grew one. I have an athletic build, but I am slight, so I fit in pretty well with French girls. Some of my AFS friends weren't so lucky. I mentioned earlier that my friend La-grande is tall and strong, but not at all fat. Where she came from in Portland, Maine, she felt like she was of normal size, because she is. In Valence, however, she felt huge. People actually stared at her. I think the kids at Ridgefield High are probably slow to accept outsiders, too. I think socially it would be tough to come to Ridgefield. I know that it was tough to go to Emile Loubet. AFS does a good job from its side, providing activities for the kids who go to France and also to America. But nothing could adequately prepare you for the inevitable shock. Making those first, essential contacts with one's peers is frighteningly difficult, and of no importance to Valence's school system. I might have sat in my room forever if Mustapha and Colin, Leane, Marie, and Emmanuel hadn't made the unusual, unprecedented effort. Without friends, the exchange program would be too lonely for words.

EIGHT

Je Voyage
(I TRAVEL)

This is a train story. Before I came to France, the only train I had ever taken was the Metro-North commuter train from New Canaan to New York City. What I liked best about that train was that I was on it and my brother wasn't. Getting to do things first is one of the advantages of being the older sister. It's even more satisfying when the younger brother is beside himself with envy. But the train ride itself was dirty and drafty and late. My parents talk about the Pullman trains of their childhood, but most of them are gone now, or greatly changed. And it's cheaper to go by air, not to mention faster. I guess in America the trains just couldn't compete.

In France, however, the trains are beautiful, quiet, clean, and fast. In five months I have traveled thousands of miles on trains. I like air travel because it's fast. It's exciting every time I fly because an airplane travels great distances in so little time. You can board a plane in New York in a blizzard and step off three hours later in Miami or Dallas into warm sunshine. Getting there isn't fun, though. It's a long ride by car to the airports, and expensive. Airports are big and uncomfortable and not very user-friendly. You are instructed to arrive hours before your flight for the convenience of everyone but the traveler. Then you are expected to wait patiently in long lines in order to check your luggage, be herded through metal detectors, get your boarding pass, and find your cramped seat. You may or may not take off on time, or anywhere near it. And once in the air you see little or nothing of the earth beneath.

On French trains, getting there is half the fun of the travel experience. Train stations are conveniently located in the center of town. If you don't have a ride, buses to the stations are reliable and inexpensive. Some train stations are nicer than others, but there's always a place to sit and read. If you travel on the Bullet Train, you need reservations, but on other trains, you can buy your ticket the day of your trip or, if you wish, on the train. You can choose which class of travel you want or can afford, but anyone can move freely within the train, and no traveler is uncomfortable. A porter will carry your baggage for you. If you travel first-class, you can eat real food at a real table with a tablecloth and crystal. And a waiter serves your meal. But this costs 240 francs, or 48 dollars, which is a lot for glorified airplane food. No matter what class you travel in, you can choose to bring your own food or buy it in the bar car, where it is not as tasty, but reasonably priced. By far the best deal is to buy your lunch at a bakery or sandwich shop right before you board the train. For $5.00 or less you can buy a freshly baked foot-long baguette with your choice of fillings: ham and cheese, marinated vegetables, tomatoes and brie, or tuna salad, chips, and a soft drink or a beer. My brother-in-law reports, however, that he and my sister were treated rudely by the first-class stewardess, who took offense when they took up space in her car without buying her $48.00 lunch. So you buy those baguettes at your own peril if you travel first-class. However you choose to travel, the best part is that these trains, which are superior in every way to American trains, are cheaper than air travel within Europe.

And once in motion, you can see the changing patterns of the landscape. Although small by American standards, France is actually a big country, and its different regions vary dramatically. The Ardêche, which is near my home in Valence, is a land of deep gorges, rugged mountains, and winding rivers. Undiscovered by the foreign tourists who crowd into Provence in the spring and summer, it's the French who vacation in the Ardêche. South of the Ardêche is the Languedoc and Provence, where the Maritime Alps overlook the blue Mediterranean. Here there are vineyards, tiny medieval villages barely sticking to steep hilltops, and fields of sunflowers and lavender. I have left Valence in a snowstorm and gone cliff climbing a few hours later near Nîmes in a T-shirt and barefoot, stepping carefully to avoid the cactus on the mountainside. North of Valence I've seen the Rhône river valley up to Lyon, the *gastronomique* capital of France, and to the east are the magnificent French Alps. The train also weaves through the world famous wine-growing regions of Burgundy and Champagne, before concluding its journey in Paris. My country is so big that a traveler cannot see it all by train unless he has months to spend. But France is accessible by train, and it would be a shame to fly over it. I am grateful that I have months to spend, riding on trains.

As I have become more comfortable in my adopted country and fluent in its language, I also enjoy train travel for the opportunities it gives me to observe other travelers, listen to their conversations, and try to imagine where and why they are traveling. Occasionally something happens which is quite unexpected and joyful. After one school holiday my host mom and I were at a train station in Lyon. She left to take a walk, and I submerged myself in a French novel. I'd been in England for ten days, and I needed to get my brain back in the French groove. The empty seat next to me was taken quickly by an attractive but weary-looking traveler. She was about twenty years old, I guessed, and probably not French. I watched her sneakily while I pretended to read. She took some postcards out of her purse and began to address them. Her handwriting was small, so it was a real challenge to read it while appearing to look at my book, but somehow I managed without actually falling into her lap.

The address she wrote was Hamilton, New Zealand. I actually know someone from Hamilton. Before I went to

France all I knew about New Zealand was that it is somewhere near Australia. Now I have two AFS friends who are
natives of New Zealand.

Suddenly the world was very small, and I couldn't contain
my curiosity. I spoke up. "You come from New Zealand?" I
asked.

She jumped, and then turned to look at me. "I thought
you were French," she said, "because I heard you talking to
someone in French."

YES! I thought. All foreign exchange students live for the
moment they are mistaken for natives. (I decided to ignore
the fact that the first person to mistake *me* for French was
English-speaking.)

I responded that I was an American student living and
going to high school in France. We agreed it was nice to
have someone to talk to while we waited for our trains,
going in opposite directions. She had been visiting relatives
in France for the holiday, she said. She added that one was
her sister, who is also going to school in this country. It was
then that I got a funny feeling, and I really looked at my
fellow traveler for the first time. The resemblance was
there for sure. "Your sister's name is Renée, isn't it?" I
asked. "And she's living in Valence." She was suitably
impressed. In fact, she was struck dumb. I am not psychic.
Renée, as it turns out, is a good friend of mine. I knew that
her sister was coming to France for Christmas, and both
Renée and I were upset because my travel plans prevented

me from meeting her sister. Or did they? Actually our travel plans drew us together at the same moment, in a city neither of us had been to before, when we happened to take adjoining chairs in a train station. We talked for an hour, like old friends, both knowing we would probably not cross paths again.

NINE

L'Escalade
(ROCK CLIMBING)

*V*ive les vacances! The juniors spent only one week in school in the month of April, owing to BAC preparations at lycée Loubet. At this time of year, the seniors spend weeks taking pre-BAC tests to prepare themselves for the rigors of the real exams. The school building is relatively small, so all the available space is taken up with suffering students and their whip-cracking professors. This happens every year, but nobody bothered to tell the foreign exchange students. Perhaps they assumed we knew in advance or would just figure it out. Never overestimate a foreign exchange student. At first I was clueless. Then I was amazed. And finally, I was thrilled. It is assumed by the school officials, of course, that everyone will either stay at home or flock to the library to cram as many hours of studying as possible into the extra time. Well, not exactly everyone. Those of us with weak brains and weaker resolve are heading for the hills—the Massif Central to be precise. My escalade club is back in business now that the snow is gone from the local mountains, and there is no shortage of local climbers.

Spring comes early to the south of France. By the end of March the fruit trees flower in pink and white along the Rhône valley, and by early April the world is green again. The sky is a brilliant cobalt blue. What the travel photos don't show is the wind. It never ceases to blow. It comes out of the north, picks up speed in Valence, and roars down the valley all the way to the sea. This is no breeze. It howls. And it makes the air feel much colder than it is. I lived in France for eleven months, and the mistral blew the entire time. I could tell it was going to be a mild day when I was strong enough to push my shutters open against the wind. This was a mild April day—a perfect day for rock climbing.

Valence is encircled by mountains. A dedicated climber can get to a challenging site in as little as fifteen minutes. And while some things, like clothes, are ridiculously expensive in France, escalade is cheap. For about $40.00, a person can join a club and climb for eight months of the year. The club provides the transportation, ropes, metal rings, and safety belts. All I had to buy were the shorts and proper shoes. The Massif Central range, which was in my backyard, is older and more worn down than the Alps. That is not to say these cliffs aren't challenging. Some of them have a three-thousand-foot vertical drop, which is plenty for me.

On this day my friends and I met in town because we were going to take a bus to a site thirty minutes away. We were a sight ourselves, dressed in spandex shorts and windbreakers, with huge packs on our backs and coils of rope around our necks. Probably we wouldn't attract too much attention on Main Street in my hometown because Mountain Workshop is right around the corner. This is the group that introduced me to rock climbing five years ago. But in Valence we attracted attention. There people dress semiformally to pick up the mail. Once I even saw a very pregnant woman trying to walk down the side of a mountain in high heels. And I was the only person who thought she looked a little bit out of place.

On this occasion the bus took us to St. Peray, where we hiked to the foot of the mountain range. From there it is a forty-five-minute climb to the cliffs we planned to scale. Before we could attack the cliffs, however, we stopped for a cookie break. This is a required part of any outdoor adventure in France. The French consume an unimaginable quantity of sugar. Nothing is too sweet for them, too rich, or too chocolaty. I made many difficult cultural adjustments during my year abroad. This was not one of them. We gave our blood sugar a jolt and began the trek.

Climbers work in teams of two, with one in control of the rope which secures the other. This buddy system assures that a climber won't fall if she loses her grip. Although it looks death-defying and frequently feels that way, the system is actually quite safe, once you've learned how to use the equipment and have mastered a half dozen climbing knots. Knowing that intellectually, however, is small comfort when you find yourself on a sheer rock face with nothing between you and a dizzying drop of a thousand feet or more but tiny cracks and bumps in the vertical surface of the stone. Fear is the enemy you have to push constantly to the back of your mind. Climbing is a mental exercise as much as a test of physical endurance. It is an exercise in self-control and concentration. Hanging there and inching your way up, you have to know precisely what both feet and both hands are doing—in other words, to think of four things at once. Trust is the other essential component of the sport. You must trust the judgment and skill and concentration of your teammate completely. You literally cannot function without each other, so you have to give as much thought to the other person's safety and mental state as your own. We all know how easy that is, especially when your life is literally on the line!

I love this sport. Adrenaline surges through your body, and it keeps pumping because we all have a primitive fear of falling. Every muscle of your body tenses; your hands sweat as you search for the next grip, which is never as close or as good as you'd like it to be. The key is to keep moving. If you hesitate, you end up completely drained of strength, both mental and physical, and then fear takes over. But if you keep going, something wonderful happens. You get to the top. Then you can secure yourself to the permanent chain and allow your arms and legs to hang loose. As all the tenseness leaves your body, you turn your head away from the dull rock face into an explosion of light and color. For a moment it is as if the world just came into being. There is

France lying far below you, vast, untouched, and silent. You enjoy the view from the top of the world, and you feel a sense of pride in a job well-done. But you don't get much time to pat yourself on the back, because the moment is broken by your partner's voice. She is eager to reverse the positions. So you take one last look, push off, and rappel to the ground—slam, bang back to earth.

My year in France was a lot like rock climbing. The journey was long and slow, and the footholds small and hard to find, but by late April the end was in sight, and in my mind I had begun the swift and exhilarating descent. Looking down from the top, I knew that my view of the world would be changed forever, and so would I.

TEN

Les Chiens Français

(FRENCH DOGS)

No story of a year in France would be complete without a chapter on French dogs and their people. French dogs accompany their families wherever they go. They travel on trains and on buses and in taxicabs. I haven't flown with a dog in the passenger cabin, but it would not surprise me to be seated next to one—not in France anyhow. And it didn't startle me to see dogs in boutiques and markets, *parfumeries*, *pâtisseries*, and *tabacs*.

A dog at the hair salon, seated on the lap of his mistress and apparently reading a magazine while she sat under the hair dryer, seemed a bit unusual, but a dog seated next to you at a restaurant, now that takes a bit of getting used to.

I first saw a dog on a table at an outdoor café in early September, shortly after I arrived. It was small, and I thought it was a child's stuffed toy until it got up, stretched, and walked across the table to take in the view from another direction. Compared to the other cultural shocks I had sustained since stepping off the Bullet Train in Valence, a dog on a café table was a small matter.

If the laws of gravity had been reversed, it would hardly have been more unsettling than listening to people speak paragraphs of gibberish day after day, trying to understand and reply, failing, and watching them look at you like the village idiot. Despite the stress level, it registered somewhere that dogs don't walk on café tables in Connecticut.

And later, when I was in my right mind again, I began to focus seriously on French dogs.

The French treat their dogs in much the same way that they treat small children, with tolerance and good humor. Both are welcome anywhere their families go and are rarely disciplined. The dogs may actually be more welcome, because they show up with their masters at the finest restaurants much more frequently than small children.

Some Americans find this charming. It adds to the foreign ambience. Others allow their meal to be spoiled by their fixation on hygiene. And some are frankly horrified. My Aunt Mary belongs to the group who are charmed. My grandma travels everywhere with a can of Lysol in her purse, so you know how thrilled she was with her canine dinner partners. The dogs in France don't always lie under the table. Depending on their size, they sit beside their owner on the floor, in his or her lap at the table, or, if there is room, at the table in chairs. Sometimes they eat dinner. A friend of my family's, who travels frequently to Paris, says he eats at a restaurant where the chef prepares a meal nightly for an old Frenchman—and his dog. On one occasion, when my Aunt

Mary was staying at a hotel in Valence, she asked if she could photograph a particularly pretty Bichon Frisé dining with his family at the next table. *Bien sûr, Madame,* said the gracious owner. And with that, he picked up the dog, cleared a space, and set it on the white linen tablecloth. Then he motioned the waiter to stand aside for a moment so my aunt could get a clear shot of his glorious pet.

The dogs in my host family were treated no differently. After their people left for work and school, they draped themselves across their favorite chairs for their morning nap, which, sometimes without interruption, ran right into their midday snooze. Then, at last, they roused themselves in the late afternoon to greet the family before a leisurely dinner at the dining-room table. Because of his size, the yellow Lab was restricted to the sofa, but the poodle sat behind my host mom at the dinner table. She is petite, but she still had to perch at the edge of her chair to make sure the beast had enough room to be perfectly comfortable. Nothing changed when the family entertained, except that the family dressed semiformally. The guests seemed to take it for granted that animals would be hanging off all the furniture. Some people even chatted with the dogs during dinner. As a foreigner it is unsettling when you are unsure whether a guest is addressing you or the lower mammal seated next to you. In the beginning I didn't mind because the animals had a larger vocabulary than I did, but later I found it a bit offensive.

My mom would love France. At home we've caught

her discussing everything from presidential politics to the vanishing rain forest with our black Lab, who always shares her viewpoint. Not that I have a problem with this behavior. Dogs have warmed my feet through the long Connecticut winters as long as I can remember. Restaurants, however, are another whole level of dog madness. I should be careful to point out, though, that French dogs are perfectly behaved in public places, from the boulevards and parks to the three-star restaurant Pic in Valence. There my Aunt Anne and Uncle Tom had the privilege of dining with several dogs, seated with their "families." The dogs were quiet and well mannered. The people were, too, of course, but one expects that.

My favorite dog diners were at a restaurant named *Le Chien Qui Fume* (The Smoking Dog) in Paris. There we were seated near a serious couple with long noses, each of whom had a dachshund on his/her lap. The dogs were so still that we didn't notice them at first, but occasionally they stretched their necks and brought their long noses up to the tabletop, like periscopes. Later, it became clear what they were waiting for—the ice-cream course. When at last it arrived they stood up on their little legs and placed their heads on the table, expectantly. It looked like a routine which the four of them had gone through many times before. And in Gordes, at a lovely restaurant overlooking a gorge, there was a group of eight people and two dogs. I had my back to the table, but my mother and brother-in-law,

John, saw one of the women putting food under the table at regular intervals. It wasn't until she rose to leave, and the animal stood up, too, that they realized that it was a St. Bernard, whose back was as high as the table and who must have weighed 175 pounds. He never moved or made a sound for the two and a half hours that they spent at dinner.

I shudder to think what would happen if Travis, my Lab, who is only eighty-five pounds, was let loose inside Stonehenge or Le Château, two restaurants near my home in Connecticut. And if he saw the deer grazing outside Le Château, nothing would be left standing in his path, including the window. My dog acts like a dog. French dogs are unnatural. My dog treed a cat once on top of a Christmas tree decorated with dog bones in the vet's office. After the tree fell down and he chased Henry (the cat) up the back stairs, he ate the dog bones. That's what dogs do. It's in their nature.

And dogs drool when they see food. They can't help it. Drooling is programmed in their genes. French dogs do none of these lowly things; certainly not when they are eating out. They wait politely to be offered a morsel of food, and when they are rewarded, they don't take your fingers with the snack. Their lips touch you as gently as a butterfly's wing.

Perhaps French dogs are more highly evolved than American dogs. The French would have you think so. But then the French would have you believe *they* are more highly evolved as well.

ELEVEN

Le Jour
(THE DAY)

As *summer arrived in France,* and I realized I was approaching the end of my journey, I began to think about all I had done and become, and to wonder what effect this year abroad would have on my life. My Webster's says that, originally, a journey was the distance traveled in a day, or *jour.* Later it came to mean a trip or travel from one place to another that might, in fact, take many days to accomplish. Mine was a journey of over three hundred days. I arrived in Paris on September 1 and the last day of school was June 16.

On June 20, I met my family in Paris. I had not seen my mom and dad or my brother, Tim, for nearly ten months. I don't know how to write about that moment. It was powerful and joyful. I was no longer alone. I was safe and secure again. We were all in the mood for a celebration, and Paris provided just what we were looking for. June 21 is the annual celebration of the summer solstice, the longest day of the year. On that night Paris doesn't sleep. Beginning about 9:00 P.M. and continuing until dawn, the entire city rings with music, from the French Philharmonic Orchestra in the courtyard of the Louvre to jazz in the Latin Quarter, hard rock in Montmartre, and madrigal singers on the rue de Rivoli.

The French riot police began arriving around noon and by dinnertime they were everywhere, looking official and intimidating in dark blue uniforms with black boots and rifles across their backs. There may have even been a riot somewhere, but everybody we saw was there for the music. As night fell, my brother and I sat on the Pont Neuf and watched the lights come on down the length of the Seine and beyond in the Eiffel Tower. The tour boats, called *mouches* or flies, because they are thick as flies on the river in summer, sparkled with party lights, and we heard laughter and music as they sailed under the dark bridge. Then we crossed over to the Left Bank, where the students live, and joined the celebration.

From Paris we took the Bullet Train to Avignon and from there we drove to our rental house in Bonnieux, a tiny hill town in Provence. It was an old stone farmhouse with whitewashed walls, terra-cotta floors, and exposed beams in the ceilings. The French farmers knew what they were doing. The thick stones felt cool to the touch and kept the interior comfortable even on the hottest days. The wooden shutters were painted that Mediterranean blue called *azur*, which reflects the color of the afternoon sky in Provence.

On the morning of my three hundredth day in France I sat on the stone fence and watched the early-morning light touch the bell tower of the eleventh-century church at the top of Bonnieux. After thinking about it for months, I might have missed the moment entirely, except that I heard my mother leave for the bakery to get our day's supply of croissants. She was compulsive about getting there early so they wouldn't be sold out of *pain au chocolat*—the favorite of all the kids.

I was tempted to stay in bed, but I padded downstairs barefoot and went outside to wait for my mother to return. In the sunlight, the village looked white. It was actually the pale sand color of the earth and stone from which it was built almost a thousand years ago. As it shimmered in the sun, it looked like a mirage.

I had completed a journey of three hundred days in France, and that, too, seemed almost like a dream. As I sat alone with my toes curled in the coarse grass, I realized I was there because I needed to begin to sort out my thoughts. I needed to begin to understand what it was all about.

What had my journey meant, anyhow?

My trusty Webster's tells me that a journey can be "an often extended experience that provides new information or knowledge beyond that which one might normally acquire. . . as in a journey of faith, or into the customs of another country." How did he know? I left a life that was predictable, comfortable, and as rhythmic as time itself, and journeyed to a place that was unpredictable and uncomfortable, where the rhythms of life were jarringly altered. Along the way I acquired a second language, *traveled*, came to understand the people and customs of another country, *traveled*, spent an entire school year at a French lycée (and lived to tell about it), made French friends I hope to have for a lifetime, other friends from all over the world, and plans to *travel* even more to visit them all.

I think I can safely say that if I had not made this journey, I would not have accomplished any of these things. I also would not have experienced homesickness so profound there are no words to describe it, and some failures so humiliating that the words to describe them are not used in polite company.

For example, let me tell you about my first day of school. School started on my tenth day in France. My host mother dropped me off at the lycée. I had never seen the building before. The principal left me alone outside a classroom. I had no idea what to do. I didn't know that I stayed with this group of twenty-four people all day. I did not know my schedule, how long the class periods were, or that my teachers were unaware that I was attending their class for the whole year. I went inside. No one greeted me. I sat through the class, which was an hour long. I was acutely aware of my breathing, which was fast and shallow. I felt like I couldn't get enough air. I wanted to bolt and run. Finally it was over.

When the bell rang, everyone got up and walked out. I watched, having no idea what to do or where my next class was. The teacher told me in English to follow the others.

The students walked out into a courtyard. They all lit up. It was the longest ten minutes of my life. I stood there, alone, trying to smile and look occupied, while the others talked and ignored me completely. I memorized a face from the first class and never let that person out of my sight. The bell sounded again; we filed in. I followed the face to the right room. It was at that point that Mustapha noticed me—that I was still there. He decided to help the stranger.

He is from Morocco and speaks English well. He told me not to take it personally that no one would speak to me, because they would treat anyone who wasn't a native of Valence the same way. Mustapha explained the layout of the building and the progression of the day. When he discovered I didn't know how to get home for lunch, he even located my bus and all but pushed me on it.

At the time I had never heard of existentialism or Sartre or Camus. Now I know that this was an existential experience. I was utterly abandoned. My points of reference were erased. I could neither speak nor understand. I was the stranger. And I was furious with everyone: with the principal for providing no orientation, with the students for looking right through me, with my teachers for doing nothing to make me feel welcome, or even to introduce me, and with my host mother for not teaching me how to get to and from the school before it started. It was not an auspicious beginning.

But it was a beginning. I never consciously decided to stick it out. In fact, I fantasized a lot about running away.

What happened, I think, is that I grew up much faster than I would have if I had stayed home. I understood that if I gave up and went home, my friends and family would forgive me and soon forget, but I would not forgive myself—and I would never forget. What I have now that I didn't have before I left home is the belief that I can do anything I set my mind to do.

I don't yet understand the meaning of my journey. Perhaps the answers will come to me slowly, over time. I do know that what I gained in France is far greater than anything I lost or missed out on while I was gone. I'm glad I made the journey.

TWELVE

La Pizza d'Enfer
(THE PIZZA FROM HELL)

T*he weeks that we spent* in Provence were magical. Our farmhouse was a five-minute walk from the village of Bonnieux, which except for four restaurants and one market, *Les Trois Mousquetaires*, exists in an earlier time. The restaurants cater to the tourist trade in the summer, but they are about the only concession the townspeople have made to tourism, or the twentieth century, for that matter. There are no shops selling the brightly colored provincial fabrics, pottery, or lavender sachets and soaps you see everywhere else. They don't even hold a market day in Bonnieux. And they have a two-thousand-year-old Roman bridge, *le Pont Julien*, which they keep so well hidden you can drive right over it without even realizing it. Much more than 185 kilometers separated this hill town from the France I had known for the last ten months.

Some of the farmers, however, are more enterprising than their friends in town. They realized that crazy people, mostly from Great Britain and America, but also Paris, will actually pay to rent their old farmhouses, providing they put in a small swimming pool. One of the richest people in the valley is the pool man, but the farmers aren't doing badly either. With the extra money, everyone buys a white pickup truck, which they drive at 180 kilometers an hour wherever they go, often on the wrong side of the road, because French drivers pass anyone who gets in front of them, whether they need to or not, and no matter how fast the other person is driving—and the other person is always exceeding the speed limit. When two of these pickup trucks meet in town, it is also a matter of honor that neither one gives way to the other. The streets in Bonnieux are narrow and almost vertical. In several places there are hairpin curves wide enough for two donkey carts to pass, if one of the donkeys is very thin. Generally this is where the trucks meet and refuse to yield the right-of-way. Those tourists who are even crazier than most and rent a car like we did, should avoid Bonnieux. It isn't fun backing down a cliff while two Frenchmen sit in their white pickup trucks, staring each other down.

What is fun is walking into town every night with some good friends, sitting at a café, and sharing a drink and conversation with the people of Bonnieux. I would have never discovered their charm had I not chosen to dine at the worst pizzeria in town. Never again will I pick a restaurant because its prices are cheaper than those of their next-door neighbors.

It was evening, and my family had left to dine in Menerbes, a few kilometers away. I, however, was in the best of company—*mes copines*, Léane and Marie. They had taken the train from Valence to spend three days, three last glorious days, with me in Provence. After finishing our glasses of the local *Côtes de Luberon* wine, we walked into Bonnieux for a local pizza. There are three restaurants in Bonnieux that serve Provençal pizza, which has a wafer-thin crust and a huge selection of fresh toppings. Anything goes, from the standard mozzarella cheese version to exotic creations of fresh goat cheese, roasted peppers, eggplant or zucchini, and tiny Provençal olives. Most places serve their pizzas with a bottle of olive oil flavored with garlic and herbs and a dish of tiny hot peppers. You dribble the oil over your pizza, add enough of the peppers to make your nose run, and dig in. For dessert you can cool off with dark, rich chocolate ice cream or lemon sorbet. For the equivalent of about $8.00 apiece you can enjoy a delicious, satisfying meal in Bonnieux. I know this because my dad became addicted to these Provençal pizzas and tried them in every restaurant in town. We all knew that his sudden, daily craving for French pizza was also his subtle attempt to keep the cost of dinner for four under five hundred French francs, but we didn't say anything because nothing in France, with the exception of wine from the local *cave*, (about $3.00 a bottle) is cheap.

Léane, Marie, and I wanted to economize, too, so we decided to try the cheapest pizzeria in town. Probably we should have known that there was a good reason the prices were so low, but my dad had eaten there and pronounced it satisfactory, so we sat down at one of the several empty outdoor tables. Actually, all the tables were empty, but it was still early, and nothing in town was crowded yet, so we weren't suspicious.

Our conversation was momentarily halted when the waitress approached. She didn't walk to our table so much as she lurched out the door onto the terrace. Having reached our table safely, she hung on to it with both hands, stared at the three of us, and asked, in slurred French, how many we were. After she stumbled back inside, we all tried to imitate her speech and fell into fits of laughter. When she returned with only *two* menus and spilled my drink in my lap, we should have known it was time to leave, but we were having too much fun, and besides, good old Dad said the food was OK. We wondered out loud how many glasses of local *Côtes de Luberon* she had consumed. Once we convinced her there really were three of us, our pizzas arrived speedily, and they looked delicious. We dug in. I swallowed a large bite and raised my head to look at my friends. Léane and Marie stared back, mouths full, trying to swallow. I whispered, "*La mienne est degueulasse!*" (Mine is disgusting!)

My friends were, astonishingly enough, equally horrified with the taste of their pizzas. We refused to believe our first impressions and choked down another bite—with difficulty. At this point, the waitress stumbled outside again and actually inquired if the food was good. Never in my life have I been placed in a similar circumstance. I've been served food I didn't like and food that wasn't cooked the way I wanted it, but never have I been served food that was inedible. My mother worked hard on my table manners over the years, and the rules of polite behavior are very strict in France, so I gasped, "*oui*," but my friends just stared at her. We tried to eat because we were hungry and felt obligated to make some space on our plates. I suppose we were too stunned by the taste to realize we should have refused to eat them at all. Instead we tried to improve these *things* on our plates with the condiments. Léane dribbled large amounts of oil on hers in an attempt to improve, or disguise, the flavor. I also tested this method, only to find the oil made the mess greasier, but didn't change the taste. Curious, I ate a drop of the greenish liquid off my finger. It wasn't even olive oil. We were dumbfounded. Faux olive oil, in Provence? It simply wasn't done. We gave up on eating, and started playing with our food. Marie started it all by flinging a canned mushroom into the street. Not to be outdone, Léane tucked a slice of her pizza in the base of a potted plant. Still worried about etiquette, I just watched and cracked up. At about this time we came to our senses and decided something must be said, but each of us thought someone else could surely say it better.

Meanwhile, we were becoming aware of conversation and activity at the pizzeria next door. All their tables were full of apparently happy diners. We remained the only customers at our place. Still too cowardly to make a scene on the street, we walked over and presented ourselves, and our problem, to the owner. He grinned and remarked that he and his wife had seen us approach, and joked when we chose to eat next door. He told us the owners were the town drunks, and that we weren't the first customers to complain about the food; in fact there was a cast of thousands over the years. This confused us even more. How could a restaurant run in such a fashion stay in business? Our new friend explained that it wasn't that the cook couldn't make a decent pizza, but that she couldn't make one while intoxicated, which was several nights a week. So it was possible to get edible food there. It was a matter of luck and timing. I was relieved. My father wasn't completely out of his mind.

The proprietor of the good pizzeria asked us to step next door for a drink after we finished our "meal" and, if we were interested, he would tell us the story in more detail. We agreed and resumed our seats.

The waitress, who probably saw us leave and return again to our table, ventured back outside, apparently somewhat recovered from her excesses. When she got close enough, we told her what we really thought of the pizzas, without becoming truly unpleasant. The French are masterful at insulting one another without using vulgar or obscene language, and they never fail to say, "*Madame*," "*Monsieur*," and "*merci*" while telling each other off. Still, the woman acted offended, claiming she had run a reputable pizzeria for twenty-five years, with *no complaints*. Then she offered us free desserts. Figuring the cook couldn't destroy ice cream, we accepted, ate quickly, paid, and walked straight next door. The owners joined us, opened a bottle of champagne, and toasted our continued good health, which, at the moment at least, was uncertain. Once again we were shocked, but pleasantly so, for they treated us hospitably and chatted with us as one would with old friends. We laughed at the irony of the whole situation and concluded that had we not felt compelled to confide in them our experience with the pizzas from hell, we would have never had the occasion to exchange words.

After what seemed like only a few minutes, I looked at my watch to discover it was nearly 1:00 A.M., and I hinted to my friends that we should be getting home. As we stood to leave, I noticed that the owner had slipped away. Almost immediately, he returned, lugging a huge wooden crate. I approached to say good night, and he placed his burden at my feet. At first it did not occur to us that we were being offered this box as a gift. I glanced down to view its contents—a mixture of perhaps fifty exquisite tomatoes and ten grapefruit. "Take them!" our new acquaintance insisted, and with that his wife gave us cooking suggestions for the tomatoes. I attempted to explain that their generosity was completely unnecessary, but they remained adamant. "I have four more crates as full as this, and they'll spoil before I can use them all," he insisted.

He wanted to prove that not all the residents of Bonnieux treated visitors as his neighbors next door did. He succeeded, but he did more than that. For the rest of my life I'll have a story to tell to anyone who believes that all French people act superior, aloof, and arrogant. In a year in France I met some French people who were all of those things, but all French people don't fit that description any more than all Americans are fat and loud. It is hard to imagine more charming people anywhere than these villagers of Bonnieux. We even exchanged addresses!

We thanked them for the fruit and vegetables and set off for our rental house. Marie took one end of the crate, and I the other, with Léane in the middle to balance things. To anyone who passed us on the road in the moonlight, we must have been quite a sight, singing and trying to skip down the steep gravel road with our strange cargo. As we paused to change positions and get a better grip on the crate, I happened to glance over my left shoulder at the sky. It was then that I saw the most beautifully strange moon that ever was. I stopped short in my tracks. Léane, who had taken over for Marie, urged me on, but then she looked in the direction of my head and slowly put the crate down in the road. We stood, silent and motionless in the presence of the power of nature. The moon was a massive, glowing, salmon red ball, hanging heavily just over the horizon. Its size and fiery color made us wonder at first if it was even the moon. Could it be the sunrise? But since it did not illuminate the sky, we concluded that it was some rare effect of the Provençal atmosphere on the moon. Hastily, we returned to the farmhouse, placing our gifts on the kitchen floor, and tripping over each other to take in the view from the stone wall which enclosed the property. Motionless, we watched. Silently the moon continued its journey, just touching the treetops, a huge ball of burnt orange against the night sky. We watched until it disappeared behind the mountains. None of us spoke as we slowly walked inside and up to our beds. Provence had given me many gifts to remember that night: the town of Bonnieux, time with my friends, and the moon.